Rethinking Letter Grades

A Five-Step Approach for Aligning Letter Grades to Learning Standards

Second Edition

Rethinking
Letter Grades

A Five-Step Approach for Aligning
Letter Grades to Learning Standards

Second Edition

Caren Cameron
Kathleen Gregory

PORTAGE & MAIN PRESS

Portage & Main Press gratefully acknowledges the financial support of the Province of Manitoba through the Department of Sport, Culture and Heritage and the Manitoba Book Publishing Tax Credit, and the Government of Canada through the Canada Book Fund (CBF) for our publishing activities.

Printed and bound in Canada by Friesens
Cover and interior design by Relish New Brand Experience Inc.

Library and Archives Canada Cataloguing in Publication

Cameron, Caren, 1949-, author

Rethinking letter grades : a five-step approach for aligning letter
grades to learning standards/Caren Cameron, Kathleen Gregory. -- 2nd edition.

Includes bibliographical references.
Issued in print and electronic formats.

ISBN 978-1-55379-537-7 (pbk.).--ISBN 978-1-55379-538-4 (pdf)

1. Students--Rating of. 2. Grading and marking (Students).
3. Educational tests and measurements. 4. Education--Standards.

I. Gregory, Kathleen, author II. Title.

LB3060.37.C34 2014 371.27'2 C2014-905914-0
C2014-905915-9

22 21 20 19   5 6 7 8 9

www.portageandmainpress.com
Winnipeg, Manitoba
Treaty 1 Territory and homeland of the Métis Nation

For WRK

Who never missed a chance to remind us to

- relax – change comes in stages
- offer a step that edges away from letter grades
- keep the main message on learning
- know that the time is coming when conversations will replace letter grades
- write your experiences to help make it happen

Contents

Introduction

Who Is This Book For?

This book is for anyone who is required to determine an overall letter grade for a report card. If part of your job is to evaluate (make a judgment) and assign a grade in the form of a letter (*A/B/C*), a symbol (+/−/√), a phrase *(meets expectations/fully meets expectations/exceeds expectations)*, or a scale point (3 − 2 − 1), then this book is written for you.

What Is This Book About?

This book is about assigning letter grades. We offer one way of arriving at letter grades for summary reporting that moves away from collecting a string of marks and calculating a grade, to examining a wide variety of data and matching this evidence with a description of achievement. The approach we describe shows how to arrive at letter grades in a way that

- makes clear links to learning standards
- promotes the use of a wide variety of evidence (both quantitative and qualitative)
- shows students the learning that underlies the letter grade
- provides a bridge between assessment *for* learning and assessment *of* learning
- acknowledges the complexity of the process

This book is about arriving at letter grades in a way that brings them closer to the learning and clearly shows the achievement of students in relation to prescribed learning standards.

This book is *not* about many of the contentious issues related to grading, such as: What are grades for? Are letter grades a fit for the twenty-first century? What do parents and guardians want from letter grades? What do universities expect?

As the topic of letter grades can be so overwhelming, we have focussed on a single aspect: how to determine an overall grade for a report card.

A NOTE ABOUT TERMINOLOGY: In this book, we use the term *learning standards* to refer to what students are expected to learn and be able to do. Other terms often used include *outcomes, standards, prescribed learning outcomes.*

Why Use a Different Approach? Why Now?

Moving away from a "totalling-up" approach for arriving at letter grades was a slow process. For us, it evolved over time – and it continues to evolve. Changes in curriculum requirements, research information, and our own teaching practices pushed us to question and to rethink how we determined final letter grades for report cards.

The following key changes over the last three decades influenced our thinking:

1. **Changing to standards-based learning and grading.** A significant change was the introduction of standards-based learning and standards-based grading in the mid 1990s. Learning standards, typically defined as what all students are expected to learn and be able to do, became the point of reference for determining letter grades.

   This change was taking place across Canada and in many other countries, including Scotland, Australia, New Zealand, and the USA (see additional information in links given to education websites for these countries in the references at the end of this chapter).

2. **Changing the type of evidence we collect:** As we discovered more about how students learn in different ways (see: Gardner 1983; Armstrong 1994) the evidence of learning that we collected moved beyond assignments and tests. We started using rating scales, scoring keys, rubrics, test scores, observation records, discussion notes, symbols, and portfolio collections to indicate the quality of learning that students had done. There came a point when it became impossible to simply add up a string of numbers.

3. **Changing the mindset of learners demotivated by grades:** Our growing concern for students demotivated by letter grades was increasing (see: Kohn 1993; Guskey 1994; Stiggins 1997). We wanted to leave all our struggling learners with hope to continue to learn. We were determined to find an approach to arriving at letter grades that could help our learners move away from an "I-can't-do-it" mindset to a "growth" mindset (Dweck 2006) and be able to recognize their own strengths and areas that needed improvement.

4. **Changing the purpose of assessment:** Researchers Paul Black and Dylan Wiliam, in their article "Inside the Black Box" (1998) informed teachers around the world that the best way to increase the achievement of all learners (especially those who struggle) is to spend more time on assessment-*for*-learning practices. Our students' success with these assessment-*for*-learning practices led us to search for ways to spend more time on assessment *for* learning and less on measuring. The main purpose of assessment and evaluation had started to shift away from measuring and sorting students to supporting their learning and helping them to succeed (see Kaser and Halbert 2008).

How Is This Book Organized?

This book is organized into five chapters. In chapter 1, "Focus on Numbers," we describe our dissatisfaction with our overreliance on numbers for arriving at letter grades. In chapter 2, "Focus on Learning," we outline a five-step process for arriving at letter grades that links learning standards to letter grades. In chapter 3, "Focus on Working It Through," we take you through the five-step process, one step at a time. In chapter 4, "Focus on Questions," we respond to a dozen most frequently asked questions and have included Conversation Cards to encourage your discussion and debate. In chapter 5, "Focus on Personal Findings," we summarize seven personal findings and three reminders that we believe are worth repeating.

NOTE: The references that relate to a chapter appear at the end of that chapter.

What Are Our Intentions for Writing This Book?

We tell our stories and ideas about the contentious topic of letter grades to encourage you to think and talk more about how you arrive at letter grades. It is our intention that after reading this book you will be able to explain to colleagues a five-step process for arriving at standards-based letter grades.

Our approach is not "the answer" or "the latest model" for everyone to follow. What we offer is an option; we know, in our profession, there is no single right way to do something that fits all teachers or all teaching situations.

A Next Step

If you can relate to anything you have read so far, keep reading.

References

Armstrong, Thomas. *Multiple Intelligences in the Classroom*. Alexandria, VA: ASCD, 1994.

British Columbia Ministry of Education.*Guidelines for Student Reporting*. Victoria, B.C: British Columbia Ministry of Education, September 1994.

Dweck, Carol. *Mindset: The New Psychology of Success*. New York: Random House, 2006.<dweck.socialpsychology.org/publications>

Black, Paul, and Dylan Wiliam. "Inside the Black Box: Raising Standards Through Classroom Assessment." London, UK: King's College London, Department of Education, February 1998. <fcoe.org/uploads/cgreenlaw/blackbox.pdf>

Gardner, Howard. *Frames of Mind: The Theory of Multiple Intelligences*. New York: Basic Books, 1983. <www.howardgardner.com/bio/bio.html>

Guskey, Thomas. "Making the Grade: What Benefits Students?" *Educational Leadership* 52, no. 2 (October 1994): 14–20. <www.ascd.org/publications/educational-leadership/oct94/vol52/num02/Making-the-Grade@-What-Benefits-Students%C2%A2.aspx>

Kaser, Linda, and Judy Halbert. "From Sorting to Learning: Developing Deep Learning in Canadian Schools." *Education Canada* 48, no. 5 (2008): 56–59. <www.cea-ace.ca/education-canada/article/sorting-learning-developing-deep-learning-canadian-schools>

Kohn, Alfie. *Punished by Rewards*. Boston: Houghton Mifflin, 1993. <www.alfiekohn.org/index.php>

Stiggins, Richard. *Student-Centered Classroom Assessment*. Upper Saddle River, NJ: Prentice Hall, 1997.

Relevant Education Websites

Canada

Rethinking Classroom Assessment with Purpose in Mind. Winnipeg: Manitoba Education, Citizenship and Youth, 2006. <www.edu.gov.mb.ca/k12/assess/wncp/rethinking_assess_mb.pdf>

Scotland

"How is the Curriculum Organized?" Education Scotland. <www.educationscotland.gov.uk/thecurriculum/howisthecurriculumorganised/index.asp>

Australia

"New South Wales Primary Foundation Statements." Board of Studies, New South Wales. <k6.boardofstudies.nsw.edu.au/go/foundation-statements>

New Zealand

"National Standards and Key Competencies." Ministry of Education Curriculum Online.
    <nzcurriculum.tki.org.nz/National-Standards>

USA

"Standards-based Report Cards." Hawaii Department of Education.
    <reportcard.k12.hi.us/teachers_admin/support.htm>

Chapter 1

Arriving at Letter Grades: Focus on Numbers

In this chapter we look back at the first approach we used for arriving at letter grades, which was to focus on numbers. We scored just about everything our students did, including assignments, tests, participation, effort, projects, and homework. We gave bonus points, took marks off, added marks for participation, gave zeros – and ended up with a long string of numbers. More seemed better. Then we added, weighted, averaged, converted to percentages, and translated totals into a single letter grade. We were dissatisfied with this totalling-up approach for arriving at letter grades, but we did not know what else was possible.

To illustrate our growing dissatisfaction with this approach for arriving at letter grades, we have included our stories to encourage you to talk about your own.

Story 1: It Doesn't Add Up

At the end of the term I totalled Andrea's marks, but they didn't add up to what I knew about her learning. Andrea was definitely not a C. I looked back: my computations were all correct. She knew the course work; I saw it demonstrated every day in class. Did I weight the assignments incorrectly? Had she been away? What had I missed?

At the time I taught Andrea (Story 1), I trusted the numbers. I had little confidence in including my own observations. I worried that others (whoever they might be) would question my judgment. Numbers seemed so certain, objective, and hard to argue with. I had yet to discover that numbers do not take the place of a teacher's professional judgment.

Story 2: The More Numbers the Better!

Kevin came to me to complain about his grade in math. I'd given him a *D*, and he thought he deserved a *B*. He explained that at the start of term he "just didn't get it" but now he got it. When I looked back at his weekly quizzes and test scores, he did have low marks – until the last weeks of the term. After that, his scores were excellent. I told him I couldn't change his letter grade because when his term marks were averaged, he had failed.

I remember thinking that I had more than enough marks to justify the failing grade I had given Kevin (Story 2). I also knew that the grade did not show his actual learning. He had learned the concepts; it had just taken him longer. The grade was not right, and I knew it.

Story 3: Does Effort Count?

Jason's father came to the reporting conference to find out why his son had not received an *A* in science (his best subject the previous year). I explained that, although Jason was one of the brightest students I'd ever taught, two projects had been handed in late and three homework assignments were incomplete. Marks had to be taken off for lack of effort and for handing assignments in late. These behaviours lowered his mark to a *B*. He needed seven more points to earn an *A*.

I knew (and so did Jason and his father, Story 3) that the letter grade I had assigned Jason was not accurate. By including homework and taking off marks for handing work in late, I had distorted his actual achievement. My belief at the time was that I could control Jason's behaviour by lowering his grade. I thought it would motivate him to try harder. It didn't.

Our growing dissatisfaction with our focus on numbers caused us to look for a different approach to determine letter grades. How did other educators figure out their letter grades? We started to talk with colleagues, ask questions, and build on the shoulders of experts.

We learned that we need to think about and talk through what we did to arrive at letter grades *in the past* as a way to clear a path for a new way of reporting *today* – in the twenty-first century.

Some Key Research Findings

Observation

Y. S. Lincoln and E. G. Guba (1985) show how important it is to collect multiple sources of information, including observation, in order to provide more accurate assessment. Triangulation, as shown in figure 1.1, highlighted the importance of expanding what we collected as evidence of learning. In particular, it gave us the confidence to include our own observations as a reliable source of information.

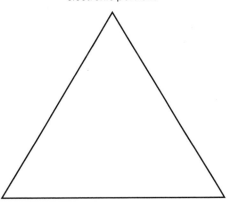

PRODUCTS
Annotated reading inventory, reading strategy grid, selected responses, text comparison, prezi, memoir, electronic portfolio

OBSERVATIONS
individual/group presentation, oral book review, writing process, listening to individuals in group work

CONVERSATIONS WITH STUDENTS
reading interview; informal conference: list of books read; writing conferences: drafts in portfolio

Figure 1.1: Triangulation – Evidence of Student Learning in English Language Arts from Three Distinct Sources

The Use of Zero

R. L. Canady and P. Hotchkiss (1989) give a list of "counterproductive grading practices," such as averaging, using zeros indiscriminately, and grading first efforts. Ken O'Connor and Rick Wormeli (2011) take a current look at the still-problematic practices of including zeros and averaging. For us, this research prompted many debates with colleagues. It was through these conversations that we were able to clarify our thinking and recognize that we had to let go of these practices to move to standard-based letter grades.

Motivation

Thomas Guskey (2011) links motivation to letter grades. He notes that "no research supports the idea that low grades prompt students to try harder. More often, low grades prompt students to withdraw from learning" (18–19). Motivation was one of the reasons we decided to rethink letter grades in the first place. This critical information confirmed what we knew to be true: All of our students are not motivated in the same way – and many students are demotivated by letter grades.

Standards-Based Letter Grades

Grant Wiggins (1998) shows how essential it is to directly connect the letter grades we assign to the prescribed learning standards: "Reports must summarize what the student has accomplished in terms that any reader outside the classroom can understand. This requires educators to provide a frame of reference … whereby outsiders can see the student's performance in some wider context" (242). Wiggins's information was essential to the development of our five-step process (see chapter 2). He pointed out that we needed to make the link between learning and letter grades clear for everyone – especially our students and our parents/guardians.

Effort

Ken O'Connor (1999) explains where effort fits in terms of letter grades: "Hard work (effort), … participation, and attitude … are all highly valued attributes, but they should not be included directly in grades because they are very difficult to define and even more difficult to measure" (47). This was a challenging idea to work through, as effort is so important to learning. O'Connor's examples helped us separate achievement from work habits and encouraged us to take another step towards increased accuracy in our letter grades.

Averaging

Robert Marzano (2000) makes it clear that averaging is not appropriate when calculating a letter grade: "An average score does not accurately reflect a student's knowledge and skill at the end of a grading period" (70). He goes on to say that "the traditional method of scoring classroom assessments using points or percentages usurps the evaluation process. That is, people rarely question whether percentage scores truly represent student learning…. Teacher judgment is replaced by the 'power of the points'"(86). This quote gave us a way to talk with colleagues and parents/guardians about the importance of not relying on numbers alone to tell the story of a student's learning.

Changing our Focus

By the 1990s, we both had made some important changes in our reporting practices. We became more selective about which numbers to include as evidence and which to leave out. Instead of blaming numbers for our dissatisfaction, we came to understand their limitations and recognized that we knew more about our learners than the numbers could show. Our overreliance on numbers had ended, and our professional judgment became more a part of the process of arriving at letter grades. Our next move was to continue to have conversations with our colleagues. The following questions helped us to continue to think about how to move away from a totalling-up approach and move towards standards-based letter grades.

 Is the achievement we are reporting on connected to the prescribed learning standards? If so, how?

What about students who can clearly explain exactly what happened in a science experiment and show that they understand the concepts but struggle to write their ideas in their lab reports? How are we supposed to assess this? How accurate are our letter grades?

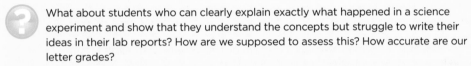 Are we leaving out important and hard-to-quantify learning standards? How do we put a number on critical thinking or teamwork skills?

How can we show clear links between the learning that has been accomplished and the letter grades assigned? For our students? For their parents?

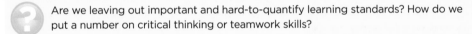 What do we do with our growing variety of assessment data, such as rubrics, student and peer reviews, informal interviews, anecdotal notes, and portfolios? How can we add all of this up?

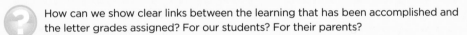 How can we help our students be clear about their specific strengths and the areas needing improvement?

In Summary

In this chapter we described our dissatisfaction with a focus on numbers and a totalling-up approach for arriving at letter grades. The more report cards we wrote, the more we knew that a different mathematical equation was not what we were looking for. We also summarized some key research findings that informed our thinking.

A Next Step

What are some of your stories about letter grades? What are some of your questions? If you are interested in moving away from a totalling-up approach that focusses on numbers, to a "matching" approach that focusses on learning, read chapter 2.

References

Canady, R. L., and P. Hotchkiss. "It's a Good Score! Just a Bad Grade." *Phi Delta Kappan* 71, no. 1 (September 1989): 68–71.

Guskey, Thomas. "Five Obstacles to Grading Reform." *Educational Leadership* 69, no. 3 (November 2011): 16–21. <www.ascd.org/publications/educational-leadership/nov11/vol69/num03/Five-Obstacles-to-Grading-Reform.aspx>

Lincoln, Y. S., and E. G. Guba. *Naturalistic Inquiry.* Newbury Park, CA: Sage Publications, 1985.

Marzano, Robert. *Transforming Classroom Grading.* Alexandria, VA: ASCD, 2000.

O'Connor, Ken. *The Mindful School: How to Grade for Learning.* Arlington Heights, IL: Skylight Publishing, 1999.

O'Connor, Ken, and Rick Wormeli. "Reporting Student Learning." *Educational Leadership* 69, no. 3 (November 2011): 40–44.

Wiggins, Grant. *Educative Assessment.* San Francisco: Jossey-Bass, 1998.

Chapter 2

Arriving at Letter Grades: Focus on Learning

In this chapter we provide an overview of a five-step process for arriving at standards-based letter grades. We constructed this process, over a period of years, as a direct result of our dissatisfaction with a totalling-up approach, which is described in the previous chapter. And, along with many of our colleagues, we felt frustration with the amount and the variety of evidence that we were collecting. Our grade books now contained more information on students than we knew what to do with (both qualitative and quantitative). They included test scores, project marks, percentages, rubric scales 1-2-3, checks and pluses and minuses, self- and peer assessments, checklists, comments, our observations, homework scores, portfolios, journals – and more. How could we determine the appropriate information to use to arrive at a single letter grade – one that was standards-based?

The five steps that we developed gave us a way to stop our overreliance on numbers and to focus our attention on the learning underneath the letter grade. The steps include:

Step 1: Identify three to five Big Ideas for one subject area.

Step 2: Write three levels of performance for each Big Idea.

Step 3: Identify evidence that shows student performance.

Step 4: Highlight descriptions of learning on the Learning Map.

Step 5: Determine a letter grade.

We have been using this approach for the last two decades, refining it every year for our own students, and along with colleagues, using it for various subjects from kindergarten to university level. To show what each step could look like, we include examples from British Columbia's English Language Arts draft curriculum, 2013. <https://curriculum.gov.bc.ca/sites/curriculum.gov.bc.ca/files/pdf/ela_learning_standards.pdf>

The Five-Step Process

Step 1: Identify Three to Five Big Ideas for One Subject Area

We start by asking: *What are students supposed to learn and be able to do in this subject?* Rather than looking at all the learning standards in our documents (the number can be overwhelming) we categorize them under three to five broad concepts that we call Big Ideas. These Big Ideas are not topics, such as "Egypt"; they are not assignments, such as "novel study"; they are not activities, such as "a lab report"; and they are not specific skills, such as "multiply fractions". Rather, identifying a Big Idea is something like finding the largest Russian doll into which a number of smaller dolls fit.

For example, in English you might assign a novel study, but a Big Idea would be for students to understand what they read; in social studies you might assign the topic of Egypt, but a Big Idea would be for students to understand what has been learned from people (e.g., Egyptians) who lived long ago.

We use Grade 7 English Language Arts (from the British Columbia draft curriculum, 2013) to illustrate the five-step process for arriving at standard-based letter grades.

The challenge for us is to make it clear to our students what they are expected to learn (Big Ideas) without confusing them (and their parents or guardians) by using too many words or educational jargon. Figure 2.1 shows an example of Big Ideas for Grade 7 English Language Arts. In this figure we've used the term *read* to include viewing. We've used the word *text* to include written, visual, digital and oral texts in a variety of genres: fiction, nonfiction, poetry, Aboriginal, Canadian, etc. Finally, we've used the word *respond* to include making connections to self, to others, to text and to culture by considering perspectives, voices, values, beliefs, questions and biases.

LEARNING MAP STEP 1

STUDENTS...

- Read a wide variety of text using reading and thinking strategies to increase understanding
- Respond to text as a way to increase understanding, enjoyment and appreciation of language, literature and story
- Communicate in written, visual and digital media forms for different purposes and audiences
- Use oral language to communicate ideas/information for different purposes and audiences

Figure 2.1. Step 1: Identifying Big Ideas. These are for Grade 7 English Language Arts.

Step 2: Write Three Levels of Performance for Each Big Idea

In step 2 we answer the question *What does the learning look like?* by writing descriptions of each of the Big Ideas at three levels of performance. To help us differentiate the three levels, we use our knowledge of students at their grade level, criteria for assignments, student work samples (provincial, district, school), provincial performance standards, and any other current curriculum and assessment documents we might have access to.

This step is like creating a map of the learning: we identify it as the Learning Map. In it, we include enough detail so that students (and parents) can see what they are expected to learn and what the learning can look like. This Learning Map becomes our reference point for arriving at a letter grade and helps keep our focus on the learning over the course of the term. When students ask "Am I passing?" or "Am I getting an *A?*" we can answer by showing them where they are on the Learning Map rather than giving a number. Figure 2.2 shows the beginning of a Learning Map with Big Ideas and levels of performance for Grade 7 English Language Arts.

Step 3: Identify Evidence that Shows Student Performance

In step 3, we ask the question *What type of evidence can I use to find out how well students are doing in relation to each Big Idea?* As this letter grade is for a summary report, we are not referring to our entire list of practices, pretests, or drafts, for example, that students do daily throughout a term. Instead, we select specific evidence by deciding which tasks, tests, or talks offer enough variety to best capture student achievement and which represent a student's learning as close to the end of the reporting period as possible.

Once we determine which evidence (e.g., assignments, tests, observations) best shows a student's performance in relation to each Big Idea, we record it on the Learning Map. Figure 2.3 shows the evidence that the teacher has selected and recorded on the Learning Map for each Big Idea.

English Language Arts Grade 7			
Students...	A	B	C
1. Read a wide variety of text using reading and thinking strategies to increase understanding	Read a wide variety of challenging text independently and with ease. Regularly use both reading and thinking strategies to arrive at a deep understanding of text.	Read a variety of grade level text independently. Typically use some reading and thinking strategies. Usually show accurate understanding and with some text, move to a deeper level.	Read short and direct text independently. May need support to use reading and thinking strategies. Often understand the gist of the text.
2. Respond to text as a way to increase understanding, enjoyment and appreciation of language, literature and story	Respond by making a variety of insightful connections that deepen understanding. Show enjoyment and appreciation of the importance of language/literature/story in people's lives.	Respond by making some meaningful connections that typically focus on self and others as a way to increase understanding. Show enjoyment of language/literature/story and recognize its importance to self and others.	Respond by making some connections to personal experiences as a way to strengthen understanding of text. Show some enjoyment of particular topics and texts and recognize particular aspects of language and story that are important to them.
3. Communicate in written, visual and digital media forms for different purposes and audiences	Communicate confidently and effectively in a variety of forms. Appropriately and creatively use the power of language to engage and impact audience. Consistently use conventions to clarify meaning and purpose.	Communicate successfully in many forms. Experiment with some language techniques and show an increasing awareness of audience. Follow most conventions to clarify meaning and purpose.	Communicate in an increasing number of forms. May require teacher support to try out new forms and use language features. Need reminders to use conventions so meaning and purpose are clear.
4. Use oral language to communicate ideas/information for different purposes and audiences	Communicate effectively and with confidence in a wide variety of oral settings. Listen attentively and ask relevant questions to extend conversations. Use the power of language in different ways to increase clarity of purpose and impact audience. Consistently use conventions to improve oral communication.	Communicate effectively in many different oral settings. Listen to others and use skills such as asking questions to sustain conversations. Use language in ways that hold the attention of audience and achieve purpose. Regularly use conventions to improve oral communication.	Communicate with some success in familiar oral settings. Can listen to the ideas of others and offer ideas and opinions. With teacher support, may try out new ways to use language when expressing ideas/information. Often need reminders to use conventions to clarify purpose and meaning for audience.

Figure 2.2. Step 2: Learning Map Showing Big Ideas and Levels of Performance

BIG IDEAS	English Language Arts Grade 7			
	Students...	**A**	**B**	**C**
	1. Read a wide variety of text using reading and thinking strategies to increase understanding	Read a wide variety of challenging text independently and with ease. Regularly use both reading and thinking strategies to arrive at a deep understanding of text.	Read a variety of grade level text independently. Typically use some reading and thinking strategies. Usually show accurate understanding and with some text, move to a deeper level.	Read short and direct text independently. May need support to use reading and thinking strategies. Often understand the gist of the text.
	EVIDENCE: Annotated Reading Inventory √ Reading Strategy Grid √ +			
	2. Respond to text as a way to increase understanding, enjoyment and appreciation of language, literature and story	Respond by making a variety of insightful connections that deepen understanding. Show enjoyment and appreciation of the importance of language/literature/story in people's lives.	Respond by making some meaningful connections that typically focus on self and others as a way to increase understanding. Show enjoyment of language/literature/story and recognize its importance to self and others.	Respond by making some connections to personal experiences as a way to strengthen understanding of text. Show some enjoyment of particular topics and texts and recognize particular aspects of language and story that are important to them.
	EVIDENCE: Selected response (rubric score 2) Interview (teacher notes) Text Comparison (graphic representation) 15/20			
	3. Communicate in written, visual and digital media forms for different purposes and audiences	Communicate confidently and effectively in a variety of forms. Appropriately and creatively use the power of language to engage and impact audience. Consistently use conventions to clarify meaning and purpose.	Communicate successfully in many forms. Experiment with some language techniques and show an increasing awareness of audience. Follow most conventions to clarify meaning and purpose.	Communicate in an increasing number of forms. May require teacher support to try out new forms and use language features. Need reminders to use conventions so meaning and purpose are clear.
	EVIDENCE: electronic portfolio final draft of memoir (rubric score 3) prezi: story/poem 9/10			
	4. Use oral language to communicate ideas/information for different purposes and audiences	Communicate effectively and with confidence in a wide variety of oral settings. Listen attentively and ask relevant questions to extend conversations. Use the power of language in different ways to increase clarity of purpose and impact audience. Consistently use conventions to improve oral communication.	Communicate effectively in many different oral settings. Listen to others and use skills such as asking questions to sustain conversations. Use language in ways that hold the attention of audience and achieve purpose. Regularly use conventions to improve oral communication.	Communicate with some success in familiar oral settings. Can listen to the ideas of others and offer ideas and opinions. With teacher support, may try out new ways to use language when expressing ideas/information. Often need reminders to use conventions to clarify purpose and meaning for audience.
	EVIDENCE: persuasive argument (rubric score 2) poem presentation 7/10 Listening Observation (teacher notes)			

Figure 2.3. Step 3: Selected Evidence for Each Big Idea Recorded on a Learning Map

Step 4: Highlight Descriptions of Learning on the Learning Map

In step 4 we ask, *Where is each learner in relation to the Big Ideas?* Using a copy of the Learning Map for each student, we examine the evidence selected and highlight the descriptions that most closely match the evidence for the student. Sometimes we highlight partial descriptions; sometimes we highlight part of one level and part of another level, as students are often all over the map.

We repeat this process for each of the Big Ideas. When we use the evidence to highlight the descriptions for an individual learner, it is much like plotting places on a map. Looking at the map, students see where they are supposed to be going in the first place, how far they have been able to go, and see a direction for their next step.

When we have a Learning Map highlighted for an individual student, the map becomes our basis for determining his or her letter grade. Figure 2.4 shows a highlighted Learning Map for an individual student.

Step 5: Determine a Letter Grade (and a Percentage if Necessary)

In step 5 we answer the question *Which letter grade is the closest match for each student?* by looking for patterns of student performance on the highlighted Learning Map. It is typical for students to have descriptions highlighted at more than one level of performance. We look for the pattern and use our professional judgment to determine the letter grade that is the best match.

If you are required to give a percentage (currently in British Columbia, percentages are required only at the Graduation Program level; in grades 10, 11, and 12), you can assign a letter grade first and then change it to a percentage. This can be done by assigning a range of percentage points for a low, middle or high grade (see Appendix 1, page 51, See also page 13, *Reporting Student Progress: Policy and Practice* [British Columbia Ministry of Education, 2009], for the range of percentages for each letter grade.)

Questions to Guide the Five-Step Process

Step 1: What are students supposed to learn and be able to do in this subject?

Step 2: What does the learning look like?

Step 3: What type of evidence can I use to find out how well students are doing in relation to each standard?

Step 4: Where is each learner in relation to the Big Ideas?

Step 5: Which letter grade is the closest match for each student?

English Language Arts Grade 7			
Students...	**A**	**B**	**C**
1. Read a wide variety of text using reading and thinking strategies to increase understanding	Read a wide variety of challenging text independently and with ease. Regularly use both reading and thinking strategies to arrive at a deep understanding of text.	Read a variety of grade level text independently. Typically use some reading and thinking strategies. Usually show accurate understanding and with some text, move to a deeper level.	Read short and direct text independently. May need support to use reading and thinking strategies. Often understand the gist of the text.
EVIDENCE: Annotated Reading Inventory √ Reading Strategy Grid √ +			
2. Respond to text as a way to increase understanding, enjoyment and appreciation of language, literature and story	Respond by making a variety of insightful connections that deepen understanding. Show enjoyment and appreciation of the importance of language/literature/ story in people's lives.	Respond by making some meaningful connections that typically focus on self and others as a way to increase understanding. Show enjoyment of language/literature/ story and recognize its importance to self and others.	Respond by making some connections to personal experiences as a way to strengthen understanding of text. Show some enjoyment of particular topics and texts and recognize particular aspects of language and story that are important to them.
EVIDENCE: Selected response (rubric score 2) Interview (teacher notes) Text Comparison (graphic representation) 15/20			
3. Communicate in written, visual and digital media forms for different purposes and audiences	Communicate confidently and effectively in a variety of forms. Appropriately and creatively use the power of language to engage and impact audience. Consistently use conventions to clarify meaning and purpose.	Communicate successfully in many forms. Experiment with some language techniques and show an increasing awareness of audience. Follow most conventions to clarify meaning and purpose.	Communicate in an increasing number of forms. May require teacher support to try out new forms and use language features. Need reminders to use conventions so meaning and purpose are clear.
EVIDENCE: electronic portfolio final draft of memoir (rubric score 3) prezi: story/poem 9/10			
4. Use oral language to communicate ideas/information for different purposes and audiences	Communicate effectively and with confidence in a wide variety of oral settings. Listen attentively and ask relevant questions to extend conversations. Use the power of language in different ways to increase clarity of purpose and impact audience. Consistently use conventions to improve oral communication.	Communicate effectively in many different oral settings. Listen to others and use skills such as asking questions to sustain conversations. Use language in ways that hold the attention of audience and achieve purpose. Regularly use conventions to improve oral communication.	Communicate with some success in familiar oral settings. Can listen to the ideas of others and offer ideas and opinions. With teacher support, may try out new ways to use language when expressing ideas/ information. Often need reminders to use conventions to clarify purpose and meaning for audience.
EVIDENCE: persuasive argument (rubric score 2) poem presentation 7/10 Listening Observation (teacher notes)			

(Left margin vertical text: BIG IDEAS)

Figure 2.4. Step 4: Highlighted Learning Map

In Summary

In chapter 2, we've outlined a five-step process for arriving at letter grades. We begin by categorizing learning standards under broad concepts that we call Big Ideas, develop a Learning Map, and plot student performance as a basis to determine a grade.

A Next Step

In chapter 3 we offer practical advice for working through each step. We explain some things we have learned to do, and some that we would never attempt again. If you are interested in going further and making your own Learning Maps, read on.

References

British Columbia Ministry of Education. *English Language Arts Learning Standards Draft.* Victoria, BC: British Columbia Ministry of Education, 2013. <https://curriculum.gov.bc.ca/sites/curriculum.gov.bc.ca/files/pdf/ela_learning_standards.pdf>

British Columbia Ministry of Education. *Reporting Student Progress: Policy and Practice.* Victoria, BC: British Columbia Ministry of Education, 2009. <www.bced.gov.bc.ca/classroom_assessment/09_report_student_prog.pdf>

Chapter 3

Arriving at Letter Grades: Focus on Working It Through

In this chapter we describe our experiences working through the five-step process outlined in the previous chapter. We offer ideas, clarify terms, and highlight questions based on the work we have done over the last decade with hundreds of colleagues at all levels of the school system.

Throughout this chapter we use specific examples in a variety of subject areas to show what each step could look like. As each context is unique, we present our experiences as examples or suggestions to be adapted, not as a linear procedure to be adopted.

We do understand that as a reader you might be thinking, "Just tell us the way to do it!" However, in our experience, we've learned that we only really understand what we create for ourselves.

Step 1: Identify Three to Five Big Ideas for One Subject Area

- We work with individuals, a group of colleagues, or with an entire staff. It is important to us that people choose to participate rather than be mandated to take part.

- We start with the question "What are the five Big Ideas that you expect your students to learn in …?" (choose one subject area) and invite individuals to respond in their own words from their experiences. We've learned that going directly to curriculum documents at this point can make us want to give up before we get started; it is easy to get bogged down by the sheer numbers of learning standards and/or by the specialized and complex language used in curriculum documents. Figure 3.1 shows two teachers' responses to the question "What are the five Big Ideas that you expect your students to learn in Language Arts/English?"

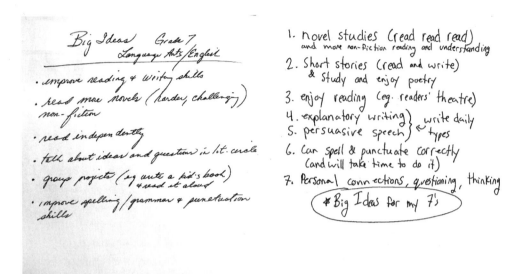

Figure 3.1: Two Teachers' Individual Lists of Big Ideas for Grade 7 English Language Arts

- As colleagues' individual lists can often focus on topics, skills, units, and activities, we stop and give an example of how their ideas fit under an overarching Big Idea. Any time we spend sharing and comparing individual lists and working together to create a combined list of Big Ideas is for us time well spent. (See Appendix 2 on page 52, where we have included Big Ideas that colleagues have created for other subject areas, such as mathematics, social studies, science, primary science, and French.) Figure 3.2 shows

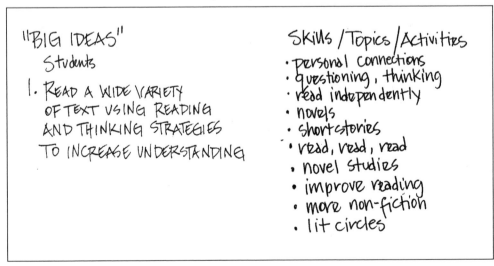

Figure 3.2: Example of How Topics, Activities, Units, and Skills Fit Under a Big Idea

how topics, activities, units and skills fit under the overarching Big Idea. Figure 3.3 shows how a group combined their individual lists and sorted them under five Big Ideas.

- Once we have identified the Big Ideas for one subject area, we then refer to our curriculum documents. To help us stay focussed on learning standards (and not get sidetracked into reading about other information, such as resources), we look at just one question: "What Big Ideas on our list do we need to add to or change?" We choose to work with hard copies rather than scrolling back and forth on the computer screen; we write directly onto the copies, cut them up, move them around, and do whatever is needed to organize our ideas.

- Reducing our list to three to five Big Ideas requires more talk time, and we find that we can move our thinking forward by asking such questions as "Is there a bigger category that these ideas could fit under?" and "Are there any ideas that we could combine with other ideas?" Given our experiences, we've learned that having fewer than three to five Big Ideas gets too general, and having more than five is overwhelming (especially in steps 4 and 5).

- The last task for step 1 is to decide on phrases that capture the gist of the Big Ideas. Since single words such as *content, knowledge,* and *skills* are too vague to identify the learning, and educational jargon such as *essential inquiries* has no meaning for students or parents, we use a short phrase that begins with a verb, such as *read* and *understand.* When it is just too hard for the group to generate these phrases together, we ask a few volunteers to have a go at bringing these Big Ideas to the group at the next meeting.

1. Read a wide variety of text using reading and thinking strategies to increase understanding

2. Respond to text as a way to increase understanding, enjoyment and appreciation of language, literature and story

3. Communicate in written, visual and digital media forms for different purposes and audiences

4. Use oral language to communicate ideas/information for different purposes and audiences

Figure 3.3: Combined and Sorted List of Big Ideas in Grade 7 English Language Arts

Step 2: Write Three Levels of Performance for Each Big Idea

- We post the three to five Big Ideas that we worked on in step 1. We've learned not to assume that people will remember what they did in a previous meeting, so we take time to read over and talk about our list of Big Ideas. These ideas are the foundations of this five-step process, and if changes need to be made, we make them now. Figure 3.4 shows the Big Ideas that were created in Step 1 and posted at beginning of Step 2.

- We put chart paper next to each Big Idea and label one chart *A*, one *B*, and one *C*. (You could use whatever symbol or phrase that you are required to use, such as *exceeds*, *meets*, or *levels 4, 3*, and *2*.) Figure 3.5 shows the placement of the chart paper with labels *A*, *B* and *C*.

- A question we typically work through first is "Why don't we describe four or five levels of performance? This would be a better fit for the letter grades we have to give (*A, B, C+, C, C-*)." At different times, we've used more than three levels. However, we've learned that we can clearly describe and differentiate among three levels of performance, but after that, it becomes difficult, if not impossible, to make distinctions among the levels.

- A related question that we spend time thinking and talking about is "Why is there no column that describes 'less than satisfactory'?" This is a challenging question because there are many different reasons

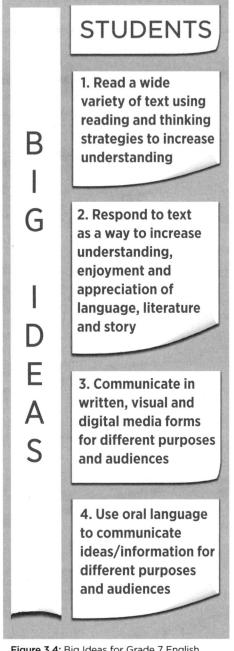

B I G   I D E A S

STUDENTS

1. Read a wide variety of text using reading and thinking strategies to increase understanding

2. Respond to text as a way to increase understanding, enjoyment and appreciation of language, literature and story

3. Communicate in written, visual and digital media forms for different purposes and audiences

4. Use oral language to communicate ideas/information for different purposes and audiences

Figure 3.4: Big Ideas for Grade 7 English Language Arts

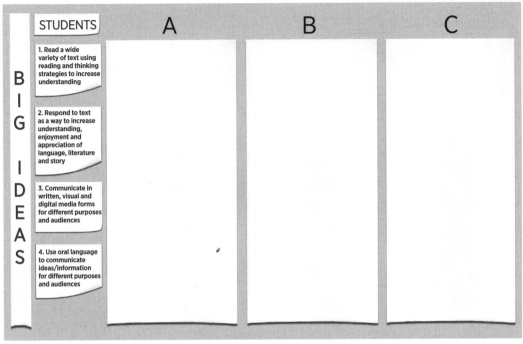

STUDENTS	A	B	C
B **I** **G** **I** **D** **E** **A** **S**	1. Read a wide variety of text using reading and thinking strategies to increase understanding 2. Respond to text as a way to increase understanding, enjoyment and appreciation of language, literature and story 3. Communicate in written, visual and digital media forms for different purposes and audiences 4. Use oral language to communicate ideas/information for different purposes and audiences		

Figure 3.5: Chart Paper Placement Showing Labels *A*, *B*, and *C*

why student performance could be less than satisfactory or not yet on the map. Some students might not have completed enough work for us to determine the level where their evidence best fits. Some might have been absent for long periods of time and others might just be beginning to learn in a particular area. We choose not to have a description of unsatisfactory performance, as students who are not yet on the map (in a particular Big Idea) often need specific plans and might require more time to learn, the reteaching of concepts, and/or individual support.

- We let students who are not yet on the map know that the description of *C* performance is what they need to be working toward. (In British Columbia, *D* or *E* letter grades are replaced with *I* (for "in progress or incomplete"). (See British Columbia Ministry of Education, 2009, 14.)

- We work on one Big Idea at a time and start by first describing the *A* (or *excellent*) level of performance in relation to Big Ideas (categories of learning standards) and then we record our thinking on the chart. To prompt our thinking, we each recall a student whose work would be considered an *A* performance, and then we talk about what that student does, says, and produces. Figure 3.6 shows a description of an *A* performance for each Big Idea.

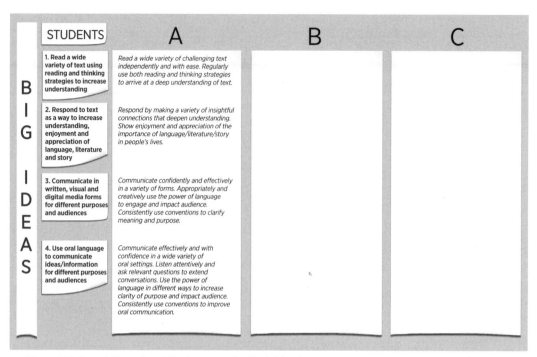

STUDENTS	A	B	C
1. Read a wide variety of text using reading and thinking strategies to increase understanding	Read a wide variety of challenging text independently and with ease. Regularly use both reading and thinking strategies to arrive at a deep understanding of text.		
2. Respond to text as a way to increase understanding, enjoyment and appreciation of language, literature and story	Respond by making a variety of insightful connections that deepen understanding. Show enjoyment and appreciation of the importance of language/literature/story in people's lives.		
3. Communicate in written, visual and digital media forms for different purposes and audiences	Communicate confidently and effectively in a variety of forms. Appropriately and creatively use the power of language to engage and impact audience. Consistently use conventions to clarify meaning and purpose.		
4. Use oral language to communicate ideas/information for different purposes and audiences	Communicate effectively and with confidence in a wide variety of oral settings. Listen attentively and ask relevant questions to extend conversations. Use the power of language in different ways to increase clarity of purpose and impact audience. Consistently use conventions to improve oral communication.		

BIG IDEAS

Figure 3.6: Description of an *A* Performance for Each Big Idea

- We repeat this process for each of the Big Ideas. In describing the *C* level, it helps us to think of a student who is "beginning to develop." To write descriptions at the *B* level, we think of a student who is strong in some areas but still needs to develop in others. It is these descriptions of learning, aligned with the Big Ideas, that form the framework for what we call Learning Maps. Figure 3.7 shows a description of an *A* performance and a *C* performance for each Big Idea. Figure 3.8 shows a Learning Map with three levels of description: *A, B,* and *C*.

- At this point in step 2, we refer to our provincial (or state) and district documents that show the range of grade-level expectations to guide our thinking as we write and revise our descriptions of learning. Learning Maps need to show the bigger picture of learning at a particular grade level, one that is beyond our individual classrooms and schools.

- Throughout step 2, we remind ourselves that the language we use to describe performance needs to be understood by our students and their parents. If any of our words have the potential to make our students feel put down, the Learning Map would end up being useless in terms of supporting learning. (See Appendix 3, page 54, which gives examples of effective descriptive language for Learning Maps.)

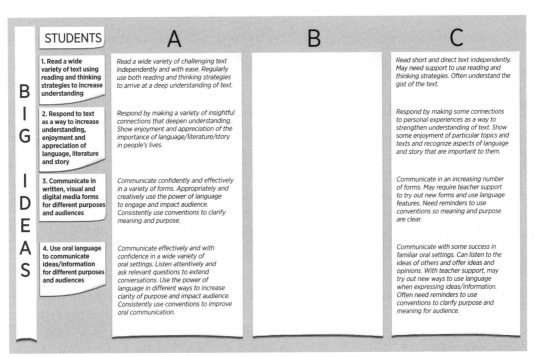

Figure 3.7: Description of a *C* Performance for Each Big Idea

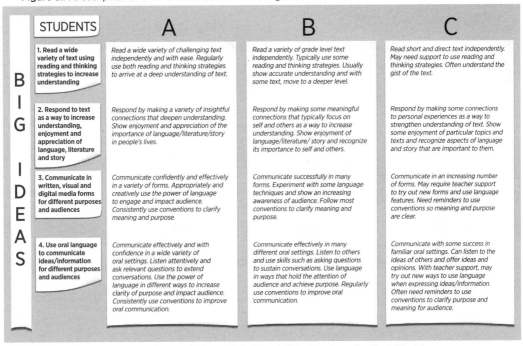

Figure 3.8: Learning Map with Descriptions of *A, B,* and *C* Performance for Each Big Idea

To complete step 2, we read through each of our descriptions and ask ourselves: "Have we left anything out? Do we need to change our language? Have we been too wordy? Are we specific enough to differentiate among levels?"

Step 3: Identify Evidence that Shows Student Performance

In order to ensure a common understanding about evidence, we start by putting the following questions on the table for discussion: "What do you mean by evidence? What evidence do we include for report cards? What evidence do we not include? Where does effort fit? How much evidence do we need?" We end up agreeing to use culminating tasks (not practices or first attempts) and typically will include one to three pieces of evidence for each Big Idea.

- We put a strip of paper underneath each Big Idea and record evidence of learning for each one. For some Big Ideas, this is an easy task; for others, it is difficult. We talk about the fact that previously our focus had often been on assignments and topics rather than on learning standards. And when we did begin to focus on learning standards, it was on the ones that were easiest to measure. For many of us, this was the first time we had actually aligned our evidence with learning standards (Big Ideas). Figure 3.9 shows the evidence selected for each Big Idea.

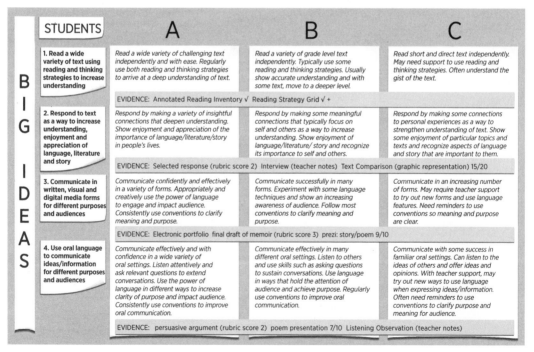

Figure 3.9: Evidence Shown for Each Big Idea

- As a last task in step 3, we take an overall look at the evidence we've recorded and ask: "Is the evidence a fit for the Big Idea (learning standard)? Have we included a variety of evidence, including products, observations, and talk with students? Have we included enough evidence for each Big Idea? Does the evidence best illustrate the student's learning? Have we gone into overkill with the amount of evidence we are including?"

Step 4: Highlight Descriptions of Learning on the Learning Map

- We try out a draft of the Learning Map, using evidence of learning from one student. At this point in step 4, we might not have actual evidence or samples of learning, so we think of one student we've taught and talk about the kinds of evidence he or she would typically produce.
- We use a highlighter pen to shade in the descriptions that best fit with his or her evidence, as shown in figure 3.10. Questions such as, "What happens when students have evidence that fits in more than one level of performance?" or "What if a student's evidence is 'between' two levels?" are typical when we are working on this step, and we need to take time to talk.

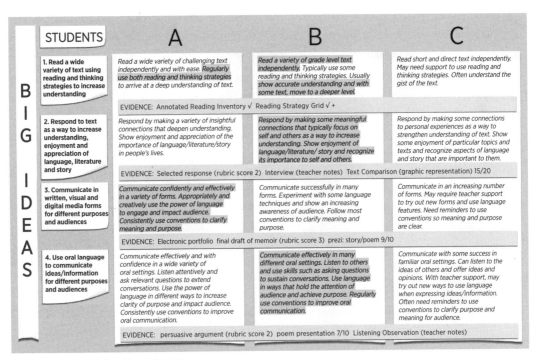

Figure 3.10: Highlighted Learning Map

- To show this range of learning, we highlight part of one description at one level and part at another. If we find it too hard to distinguish one level from another, it is at this point that we revise our descriptions and add in more detail.

- As we continue to highlight the descriptions – similar to plotting places on a map – we find ourselves looking for a pattern to emerge.

> Here's a time-saving bonus that Learning Maps provide: If you are required to assign a letter grade and provide written comments for each student, the highlighted parts of the Learning Map (along with students' specific examples) become your comments. Teachers who are not required to give letter grades have told us that they create Learning Maps (without the ranking labels *A, B, C*) to show students and parents/guardians what the required learning looks like; they use the highlighted parts of the Learning Map (which they personalize for each student) as their written report card comments.

Step 5: Determine a Letter Grade (and a Percentage if Necessary)

- We often find that we can glance at a highlighted Learning Map and easily see which overall letter grade a student will receive. But sometimes it is not so clear, and a student's performance is all over the map. Our documents remind us that making professional judgments is a part of determining a letter grade:

  From information collected through assessment activities, teachers evaluate student performance. They use their professional expertise, knowledge about learning, and experience with students, along with specific criteria, to make judgments about student performance in relation to learning outcomes [standards]. (British Columbia Ministry of Education, 2009, 21)

- The highlighted Learning Map provides us with the overall picture of an individual student's learning in one subject area. When we have completed the highlighting, we often think, "If only we could report on each of the Big Ideas, it would be so straightforward." However, as we are required to reduce all the learning a student has done to a single letter grade, we do one of the following:

  - We select the middle ground (performance) if a student's performance seems between levels or is all over the map, or

  - We look back at additional evidence that we have collected for this student, which gives us more information to bring to the Learning Map to help inform our decision

- It is essential that we use our own professional judgment to arrive at a letter grade based on the evidence we have at this time.

- If required, we assign a percentage by arriving at a letter grade first and then determining the percentage. (In British Columbia, percentages are required only in the Graduation Program grades – that is, grades 10 to 12.) Through conversations with colleagues (teams, departments, grade groups) we make a decision on which percentages will represent high, middle, or low ranges of each letter grade. (See Appendix 1 on page 51 for a sample chart from one department, English Language Arts, for determining a percentage.)

- If decisions about scholarships and awards have to be made (i.e., rankings), we ask students to complete a separate performance task, (e.g., a test or piece of written work) or present additional evidence of learning, such as a portfolio or interview.

In Summary

In this chapter we have offered questions, suggestions, and examples to help you work through the five-step process to arrive at standards-based letter grades.

A Next Step

If you are interested in finding out some of the questions and concerns that colleagues have put forward about using the five-step process, read on.

References

British Columbia Ministry of Education. *Reporting Student Progress: Policy and Practice.* Victoria, BC: British Columbia Ministry of Education, 2009. www.bced.gov.bc.ca/ classroom_assessment/09_report_student_prog.pdf>

Chapter 4

Arriving at Letter Grades: Focus on Questions

Rethinking how to arrive at letter grades is more about questions than about answers. As we stated in our introduction, this book is not about the many contentious issues related to grading. The aspect we focus on here is how to arrive at a letter grade without totalling up.

The questions that we present in this chapter are specifically about arriving at letter grades with a focus on learning; we've been asked these questions many times by teachers, administrators, parents, and our students. Some of these questions are based on longstanding beliefs and entrenched practices, while others focus on the details.

Given the scope of this book, we offer brief responses along with some favourite quotations and references that have helped our thinking. In addition, in order to encourage you to have your own discussions on this topic, we've included Conversation Cards as a way to prompt your talk, thought, and debate. (See Appendix 5, page 57.)

Questions

1. Isn't this five-step approach very subjective?

2. What do you say when parents and guardians ask for percentages? Parents and guardians see percentages as precise and more accurate than letter grades.

3. But isn't the Learning Map just another rubric?

4. Who sees the Learning Map? Is it something that is just for teachers? Or do students see it too? What about parents and guardians?

5. How can I defend my letter grades to parents and guardians? They want numbers and you're suggesting we show them a 'map'!

6. We have to use an electronic grade book. How can this five-step process work using technology? What do you do?

7. How do students react to Learning Maps? My students are just interested in their marks – "What did I get?"

8. Where does effort fit in? Isn't it a part of a letter grade?

9. How does this approach help our struggling students? So many are demotivated by letter grades.

10. What about students on an IEP? How does the five-step approach work for them?

11. How do we get everybody at our school to use the five-step approach?

12. As a principal, I want to get a discussion started around the issue of letter grades. How do you suggest we start as a staff?

Frequently Asked Questions

QUESTION 1: Isn't this five-step approach very subjective?

It was Lorrie Shepard (2000) who helped our thinking when she explained how the terms *objective* and *subjective* are left over from a time in education when behavioural objectives (rather than prescribed learning standards) focussed on rote memory and recall, and the word *objective* was used to describe tests in which students filled in the blanks, matched, and answered multiple-choice questions.

Today our curriculum requirements include problem-solving, critical thinking, mathematical reasoning, scientific open-mindedness, and willingness to question and promote discussion (to mention just a few). These learning standards require different assessment methods to measure student performance that go beyond "objective" tests and include interviews, observations and a number of other nontesting methods that some people still connect to the term *subjective*.

In the five-step approach we describe in this book, we identify the complexity of learning and show how to include a variety of evidence that goes beyond numbers to arrive at letter grades that show a concrete picture of student learning. Ruth Sutton (1997) sums it up when she says, "Whether we like it or not, assessment and evaluation is still a complex process of human judgment" (10).

QUESTION 2: What do you say when parents or guardians ask for percentages? Parents and guardians see percentages as precise and more accurate than letter grades.

Percentages may be mathematically precise, but that does not make a percentage objective or accurate. It is the teacher who decides what goes on the test, what weight will be attached to each item, and what method will be used to tally and summarize the information and arrive at a letter grade. Robert Marzano (2000) talks about the trust that people often have in a percentages: "Rarely do people question whether percentage scores truly represent student learning. They simply assume the scores are an accurate reflection of students' understanding and performance" (86).

One way that we try to have parents and guardians look beyond the number and focus on the learning is to show them the Learning Map and point out examples of their son's or daughter's learning. When we show them specific personal examples, some parents and guardians do come to understand that a percentage cannot capture the complexity of the learning, while a Learning Map points to the specific learning that their son or daughter has done and what they still need to do in order to improve. For example:

> Let's look at the Learning Map. This is what your daughter Paulina is required to learn (*pointing to the Big Ideas*). The highlighted areas show how well she is performing (*pointing to the highlighted areas*). You can see that this one area (*pointing to this section*) is a weakness, and it is holding her back from getting a better grade. A next step, which she can work on at home, is to include more details, sketches, and examples as proof that she really does understand what she is explaining. If we were just looking at a percentage of 82, this weakness might go unnoticed and you would never know these important details about Paulina's learning. And, more importantly, she might be satisfied with an 82 and not even look at the fact that there are areas she needs to work on next term.

QUESTION 3: But isn't the Learning Map just another rubric?

At first glance, a Learning Map and a rubric can look the same, as they both show levels of performance. One major difference between the Learning Map that we are describing in this book and a rubric is that the Learning Map shows the overall picture of learning in one subject area for an entire term, whereas a rubric usually describes performance in a single assignment or activity. Another difference is that a Learning Map, which is constructed by the teacher, begins with learning standards that are aligned to descriptions of performance that in turn are aligned with evidence of learning. Teachers interpret the Learning Map to arrive at a summative letter grade.

QUESTION 4: Who sees the Learning Map? Is it something that is just for teachers? Or do students see it too? What about parents and guardians?

We started out creating Learning Maps for our own use, so that we could ensure that we had aligned our prescribed learning standards with our students' evidence of learning – that is, it showed us the lay of the land. In our task of determining a summative letter grade, we *interpreted* the evidence in the maps, rather than adding it up.

For several reporting periods, because we didn't have the confidence to share them with our students and parents/guardians, we were the only ones who would see the Learning Maps. Then, when we tried them out with some parents and guardians and students, we saw the potential they had for starting conversations about the learning and decreasing the focus on the numbers.

It didn't take long, however, before showing the Learning Maps became a regular and essential part of our reporting conferences. For many parents and guardians, this was their first opportunity to see in a concrete way what standards-based reporting was all about: the alignment between what their son or daughter was to learn, the evidence selected to show it, and their level of performance for this reporting period.

QUESTION 5: How can I defend my letter grades to parents and guardians? They want numbers, and you're suggesting we show them a map!

We still use numbers to arrive at letter grades. We show parents and guardians a Learning Map that includes evidence of learning, such as test scores, marks on assignments, and presentation scores. However, a Learning Map allows us to go beyond only numbers by emphasizing the importance of linking a letter grade to required learning standards.

The Learning Map also allows us to show parents and guardians how certain prescribed learning standards require teachers to use evidence other than a number. We talk about various ways of collecting data by showing examples of our observation notes: a scale of 1 – 2 – 3 on a rubric; an interview with a student to hear his or her explanation or to evaluate oral language skills.

We've prepared a brochure that we use to help parents and guardians understand how schools need more than numbers to communicate a student's learning in the twenty-first century (see Figure 4.1 or see details in Appendix 4, pp. 55–56).

Figure 4.1: Parent Brochure: Arriving at Standards-Based Letter Grades

QUESTION 6: We have to use an electronic grade book. How can technology help us use this five-step process? What do you do?

First, we don't use any grade-book program for the purposes of totalling, averaging, ranking, converting, or deciding the letter grade. We are the teachers, and we determine the letter grade. We worry when electronic programs, in effect, become the "grade maker" and the teacher simply inputs the data without interpreting it.

However, we do use technology to track each student's overall collection of evidence, which we organize under each of the Big Ideas headings rather than under assignments and tests. In Figure 4.2, the highlighted areas show the evidence selected for assigning a letter grade at the end of the term. In Figure 4.3, note that our observations are recorded on sticky notes, dated, and placed under the Big Ideas.

BIG IDEAS			
Students...			
Read a wide variety of text using reading and thinking strategies to increase understanding	Respond to text as a way to increase understanding, enjoyment and appreciation of language, literature and story	Communicate in written, visual and digital media forms for different purposes and audiences	Use oral language to communicate ideas/ information for different purposes and audiences
Annotated Reading Inventory √	Response journal 10 entries	Electronic portfolio Variety of forms 5 completed	Group presentation: book review #1
Chapter questions (oral and written)	Selected reader response rubric score 2	Final draft Memoir rubric score 3	Discussion Circles Practice of roles
Reading Interview (use of strategies)	Interview (teacher notes)	Prezi: story/poem 9/10	Persuasive argument (rubric score 2)
Critical Attribute List	Text Comparison (graphic representation) 15/20	Poetic language features – practice 12/15	Poem Presentation 7/10
Reading Strategy Grid √+			Listening Observation (teacher notes)

Figure 4.2: Chapter 4 figure 2A evidence for one student recorded under "Big Ideas" (outcomes). Evidence selected for assigning a letter grade at the end of the term is highlighted (English Language Arts 7)

Language Arts Big Ideas

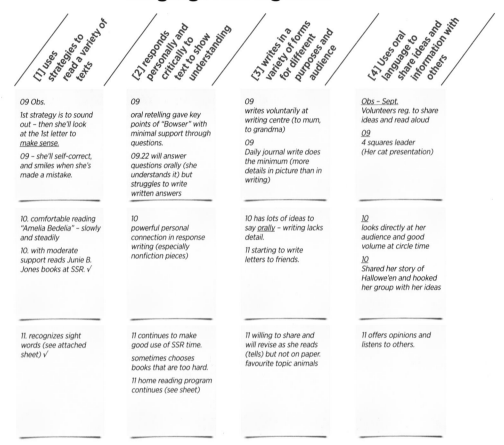

[1] uses strategies to read a variety of texts	[2] responds personally and critically to text to show understanding	[3] writes in a variety of forms for different purposes and audience	[4] Uses oral language to share ideas and information with others
09 Obs. 1st strategy is to sound out – then she'll look at the 1st letter to <u>make sense.</u> 09 – she'll self-correct, and smiles when she's made a mistake.	09 oral retelling gave key points of "Bowser" with minimal support through questions. 09.22 will answer questions orally (she understands it) but struggles to write written answers	09 writes voluntarily at writing centre (to mum, to grandma) 09 Daily journal write does the minimum (more details in picture than in writing)	<u>Obs – Sept.</u> Volunteers reg. to share ideas and read aloud <u>09</u> 4 squares leader (Her cat presentation)
10. comfortable reading "Amelia Bedelia" – slowly and steadily 10. with moderate support reads Junie B. Jones books at SSR. √	10 powerful personal connection in response writing (especially nonfiction pieces)	10 has lots of ideas to say <u>orally</u> – writing lacks detail. 11 starting to write letters to friends.	<u>10</u> looks directly at her audience and good volume at circle time <u>10</u> Shared her story of Hallowe'en and hooked her group with her ideas
11. recognizes sight words (see attached sheet) √	11 continues to make good use of SSR time. sometimes chooses books that are too hard. 11 home reading program continues (see sheet)	11 willing to share and will revise as she reads (tells) but not on paper. favourite topic animals	11 offers opinions and listens to others.

Figure 4.3: Evidence recorded on sticky notes and organized under Big Ideas (learning standards) for one primary student for September, October, and November.

We keep records of what students have done in a term – practices, assignments, redos, quizzes, tests, projects, our observations, scale marks, checkmarks – to show completion, anecdotal comments, and other assessment techniques.

In our experience, technology such as electronic grade books are good at keeping track of numbers but do not keep track of the wide variety of evidence that is needed to assess twenty-first century learning standards.

However, new assessment applications such as QUIO Learning Map have the capability of reflecting the ongoing changes that are taking place in assessment practices today.

QUESTION 7: How do students react to Learning Maps? My students are just interested in their marks – "What did I get?"

Yes, grades and marks are the currency in our school system, and we do take some responsibility for our students' focus on marks. As teachers, we've used the line "it's for marks" many a time to get the attention of the class. The point we want to emphasize is that, when using the five-step approach to arriving at letter grades, students do continue to get marks – on tests or assignments, or whenever a number makes sense as evidence. We've not stopped giving marks; we've simply stopped relying on numbers alone. And we no longer add up a string of marks to calculate a letter grade.

Using a Learning Map as the basis for determining a letter grade helps students see the learning that underlies their grade. We've seen many of our learners move beyond being interested only in their marks and begin to pay attention to and talk about the link between what they are supposed to learn (Big Ideas), how they are actually doing (evidence and highlighted descriptions of learning), and what they need to work on next.

QUESTION 8: Where does "effort" fit? Isn't it a part of a letter grade?

Effort, participation, and behaviour are important learning attributes, but they are not included in a letter grade (See O'Connor 2007, 19.) One exception is when there is a specific reference to one of these attributes, and it is stated as a prescribed learning standard, such as participation in physical education ("participate in a variety of physical activity that support their health and physical activity goals" [Physical and Health Education 7-9 British Columbia Ministry of Education draft curriculum, 2013]).

Although effort is not a component of arriving at letter grades, it is definitely something we report on. In fact, some schools make sure that this important aspect has a prominent spot on their report cards. Figure 4.4 provides a sample of the front page of a report card showing the effort of a student during a term.

A reference worth reading related to your question is Carol Dweck's research. In her book *Mindset,* Dweck emphasizes the importance of effort and its effect on learning. Another book, *Drive,* by Daniel Pink, looks at the importance of effort in everything we do in our lives.

Division 4 March 2013

Fairfield
Elementary School
1234 Treebank Rd.

REPORT CARD

Student: Colton S.

21st CENTURY HABITS OF LEARNING

To emphasize the importance of work habits, effort, and attitude in connection with learning, these 'habits' are placed front and center on the first page of this report card. Habits of learning:

- effort
- willingness to take a risk
- perseverance
- other

- work habits
- participation
- curiosity

To help students understand this powerful connection we spend time in class talking about each one of these habits and giving examples of what they could look like.

Each student has selected one habit he/she feels especially strong in and one that he/she needs to work on.

I put a lot of effort into things I like doing like reading and doing sports in the gym.

I mostly get all my work done but sometimes I don't finish my math homework.

One goal to work on: make sure I do all my math homework.

Figure 4.4: Example of a Report Card with Effort Shown in a Prominent Place

QUESTION 9: How does this five-step approach help our struggling students? So many are demotivated by letter grades.

One of the reasons we decided to rethink our approach to arriving at letter grades was our concern for students who lose hope: our strugglers.

We find that, when we use Learning Maps along with specific samples of work, the picture of what students are expected to learn and are able to do is more concrete. As a result, our struggling students start to see where their letter grade came from. Before we used Learning Maps, some students found it hard to see that they had made any progress at all. The Learning Map can show them where they did improve in some of the learning standards in a subject, even though the overall grade may have stayed the same. For example, in mathematics, an individual might have improved in computation, but his or her problem-solving is weak because the reading of the question is often confusing. So, rather than having a student think, "I am stupid in math," we point out on the Learning Map where he or she did improve in one aspect and where skills still need to be strengthened.

The issue is one of motivation. Some resources worth reading and talking about include those by Carol Dweck (2007), Daniel Pink (2009 TED Talk), and Alfie Kohn (2011). The growing awareness of the connection between motivation and letter grades gives us hope that this area of motivational research will help change the whole approach to how schools report on student progress.

QUESTION 10: What about students on an IEP? How does the five-step approach work for them?

For students who have IEPs and do receive letter grades, we make three changes on our Learning Map:

- We include the specific support or adaptation that students receive on the Learning Map.
- We focus the evidence of learning on talking with and observing learners rather than always requiring a product, such as a written task or an assignment.
- We reduce the number of Big Ideas that the student is focussing on.

Figure 4.5 shows an example of how we adapt our Learning Map for students with an IEP.

Specific adaptations used are underlined on the Learning Map

BIG IDEAS

English Language Arts Grade 7 (with Adaptations)

Students...	A	B	C
1. Read a wide variety of text using reading and thinking strategies to increase understanding	Read a wide variety of challenging text independently and with ease. Regularly use both reading and thinking strategies to arrive at a deep understanding of text.	Read a variety of grade level text independently. Typically use some reading and thinking strategies. Usually show accurate understanding and with some text, move to a deeper level.	Read short and direct text independently. May need support to use reading and thinking strategies. Often understand the gist of the text.
EVIDENCE: Annotated Reading Inventory √ Reading Strategy Grid √ -			
ADAPTATIONS: use a reader/technology • extra support for use of strategies • separate settings/scribe longer timeframe • other			
2. Respond to text as a way to increase understanding, enjoyment and appreciation of language, literature and story	Respond by making a variety of insightful connections that deepen understanding. Show enjoyment and appreciation of the importance of language/literature/story in people's lives.	Respond by making some meaningful connections that typically focus on self and others as a way to increase understanding. Show enjoyment of language/literature/story and recognize its importance to self and others.	Respond by making some connections to personal experiences as a way to strengthen understanding of text. Show some enjoyment of particular topics and texts and recognize aspects of language and story that are important to them.
EVIDENCE: Selected response (rubric score 1) Interview (teacher notes) Text Comparison (graphic representation) 11/20			
ADAPTATIONS: additional support/discussion • prompts to make connections • provide template for response use technology to record • other			
3. Communicate in written, visual and digital media forms for different purposes and audiences	Communicate confidently and effectively in a variety of forms. Appropriately and creatively use the power of language to engage and impact audience. Consistently use conventions to clarify meaning and purpose.	Communicate successfully in many forms. Experiment with some language techniques and show an increasing awareness of audience. Follow most conventions to clarify meaning and purpose	Communicate in an increasing number of forms. May require teacher support to try out new forms and use language features. Need reminders to use conventions so meaning and purpose are clear.
EVIDENCE: Electronic portfolio final draft of memoir (rubric score 1) prezi: story/poem 9/10			
ADAPTATIONS: extra time/support • talk out ideas • technology or scribe to record • extra support to edit/proofread • other			
4. Use oral language to communicate ideas/information for different purposes and audiences	Communicate effectively and with confidence in a wide variety of oral settings. Listen attentively and ask relevant questions to extend conversations. Use the power of language in different ways to increase clarity of purpose and impact audience. Consistently use conventions to improve oral communication.	Communicate effectively in many different oral settings. Listen to others and use skills such as asking questions to sustain conversations. Use language in ways that hold the attention of audience and achieve purpose. Regularly use conventions to improve oral communication	Communicate with some success in familiar oral settings. Can listen to the ideas of others and offer ideas and opinions. With teacher support, may try out new ways to use language when expressing ideas/information. Often need reminders to use conventions to clarify purpose and meaning for audience.
EVIDENCE: persuasive argument (rubric score 1) poem presentation 6/10 Listening Observation (teacher notes)			
ADAPTATIONS: Extra time and support including selected/supportive audience • Coaching in conversation groups Additional rehearsals • other			

Figure 4.5: Adapted Learning Map

For those students who have an IEP and have a modified program (not working on the prescribed learning standards of the curriculum and so do not receive letter grades), we make the following changes:

- We make the IEP goals students' Big Ideas.
- We omit step 5, as students who have an IEP with a modified program do not receive letter grades. Instead, we describe growth and progress for each of the IEP goals/individual Big Ideas on the Learning Map.

Figure 4.6 shows an example of a Learning Map for a student with an IEP who is working on a modified program.

The most important point for us is that our students who have IEPs also have Learning Maps – just like everyone else.

LEARNING MAP (Modified Program IEP Goals)				
Students...	Baseline data (Sept) Summary	By November Summary	By March Summary	By June Summary
Develop Reading Skills	Observations and notes:	Observations and notes:	Observations and notes:	Observations and notes:
EVIDENCE: samples of pages from books read; observation notes of reading aloud; student oral responses (retelling, asking questions, listening to others read); list of books he enjoys reading/being read to him				
Develop muscle tone and physical stamina				
EVIDENCE: photos/videos of student strengthening his muscles and doing his exercises; observation notes from teacher, special education assistant, physiotherapist				
Develop Social Skills				
EVIDENCE: photos/video of working with others; taking turns, using his voice, observations from teacher, special education assistant and peers				

(left margin, vertical text: BIG IDEAS)

Figure 4.6a: Modified Program Learning Map

Individual Growth and Progress tracked in summary observations and notes throughout the year and through samples in IEP Portfolio*

Figure 4.6b: IEP Portfolio which corresponds to the Learning Map, with concrete "evidence" placed in each pocket labelled with a Big Idea (related to IEP goals), e.g. work samples, photos, video etc. along with observations by teacher and special educational assistant.

QUESTION 11: How do we get everybody at our school to use the five-step approach?

We invite people to join us in rethinking how to determine letter grades, and we keep inviting them, again and again. We recognize that this approach may not be a fit for everyone. It is not an approach to mandate.

We have written this book to offer a choice, an option, for those individuals who wish to rethink how they arrive at letter grades.

QUESTION 12: As a principal, I want to get a discussion started around the issue of letter grades. How do you suggest we start as a staff?

Some colleagues who are principals have told us that one of the most helpful practices they use with staff is to set aside a 10-minute talk time at each staff meeting. Teachers work in small groups and have conversations about practices related to reporting. (See Appendix 5, page 57, for sample Conversation Cards, which can be helpful in these discussion groups).

There are also some short and thought-provoking presentations online to prompt discussion on this important topic. Two of our favourites include Dylan Wiliam, who speaks on assessment-*for*-learning strategies and Carol Dweck, who speaks about growth and fixed mindsets, giving key insights into motivation of our learners. See references at the end of this chapter.

The leaders we have worked with who surround staff with both expectation and invitation create an environment that encourages thinking, questioning, and debating. They focus on creating a safe space for talk and inquiry to happen. We've included an article in Appendix 6 (see page 60) that provides a short overview of this five-step approach that you may choose to use.

References

"Feedback on Learning – Dylan Wiliam." Journey to Excellence website: Education Scotland. <www.journeytoexcellence.org.uk/videos/expertspeakers/ feedbackonlearningdylanwiliam.asp.> This clip can also be viewed at <www.youtube.com/watch?v=n4vA2quoYio)>

Dweck, Carol. *Mindset.* New York: Ballantine Books, 2007.

and a video:

"Dr. Carol Dweck on Fixed vs. Growth Mindsets." Youtube: www.youtube.com/ watch?v=MTsF2TaEaJA>

Guskey, Thomas. *How's My Kid Doing? A Parent's Guide to Grades, Marks, and Report Cards.* San Francisco: Jossey Bass, 2002.

Kohn, Alfie. "The Case Against Grades." *Educational Leadership* 69, No.3 (November 2011), 28–33. <www.alfiekohn.org/teaching/tcag.htm>

Marzano, Robert. *Transforming Classroom Grading.* Alexandria, VA: ASCD, 2000.

O'Connor, Ken. *A Repair Kit for Grades.* Portland, Oregon: Educational Testing Service, 2007, 19–21.)

Pink, Daniel. *Drive: The Surprising Truth About What Motivates Us.* New York: Riverhead Books, 2009.

Quipped, Inc; QUIO Learning Map. <www.quio.ca>

For a quick summary for educators, see:

Pink, Daniel. TED Talk. "The Puzzle of Motivation." TED website: <www.ted.com/talks/ dan_pink_on_motivation.html> August 2009

Fliegelman, Larry. "19 Top Ideas for Education in *Drive*, by Daniel Pink". (January 5, 2011). Connected Principals website: <connectedprincipals.com/archives/2202>

von Zastrow, Claus. " 'Carrots and Sticks Are So Last Century': A Conversation with Author Dan Pink." Learning First Alliance website: <www.learningfirst.org/ carrots-and-sticks-are-so-last-century-conversation-author-dan-pink>

Shepard, Lorrie A. "The Role of Assessment in a Learning Culture." *Educational Researcher* 29, no. 7 (Oct., 2000): 4–14.

Sutton, Ruth. *The Learning School.* Salford, England: RS Publications, 1997.

Chapter 5

Rethinking Letter Grades: Focus on Personal Findings

In this final chapter we begin with three reminders related to arriving at letter grades that we believe are worth repeating. We end with a brief summary of seven personal findings that stand out for both of us as key reasons that keep us working away on this complex and emotional topic.

There is no conclusion to this book; there is only a next step. And that next step is completely up to you. We have offered our experiences, some practical ideas, and several questions to consider and talk about as you rethink how you arrive at letter grades. You decide what's next for you.

Three Reminders

Reminder 1: Letter Grades are Still a Requirement

Educators learn more about teaching and learning every year, and what students are expected to learn and be able to do continues to grow in number and complexity. Yet assigning letter grades remains much the same as it has been for over a century. If we had a choice, letter grades would no longer be a part of our system – they would be artifacts of the last century. However, as we are still required to submit final grades for summative reporting, we find the five-step approach outlined in this book is a way to put learning, rather than numbers, in the centre.

Reminder 2: There Is No Single Right Answer

The process we describe in this book for arriving at letter grades is one option, not "the answer." There is no single right way to do anything in our profession. In working with hundreds of colleagues at various levels of the system and in a variety of contexts, we have observed how the five-step approach is a good fit for some but not for others. And, all too often in our profession, we've seen exactly what can happen to a good idea when people are told that they have to "do it this way." This is not an approach to mandate.

Reminder 3: Assigning Letter Grades Is No Easy Task

We have both been teaching for over 35 years, and regardless of the approach we use, arriving at letter grades is still the most difficult part of our job. As we write this final chapter, we are in the midst of giving letter grades to our university students. We want you to know that we still worry about the letter grades we assign. We ask ourselves: "Did I assign him or her the right grade? Was the letter grade the best match to his or her true achievement? Will students question my judgment? Or is it even possible to combine so many different aspects of learning into a single symbol?" And the list goes on. Never underestimate the complexity of what is involved in arriving at a letter grade.

Seven Findings

Finding 1: Change the Conversation

It is a pleasure to have conversations at report card time with our students and their families about learning, not just about letter grades. We find that the time we used to spend justifying a grade is now spent discussing a student's next steps toward improvement. Making Learning Maps accessible to our students and their parents or guardians is the single most important thing we have done to help shift conversation from a focus on numbers and "What did I get?" to a focus on learning.

Finding 2: Expand the Evidence

We now include a wide variety of evidence about how students are performing. Our observations have become valued data. We do not leave out the hard-to-measure learning standards just because they are difficult to assign a number to. The evidence we collect gives all our students the opportunity to show what they have learned, even when they all have different ways of showing their learning. We both feel increased confidence in the accuracy of the grades we assign.

Finding 3: Remove the Mystery

We had no idea that creating a Learning Map and showing the process that we use to arrive at letter grades was so important to students. When the mystery behind letter grades is removed, some students begin to see connections between what they do in class and the grade they receive on report cards. And, when our struggling learners figure out how all of the pieces fit together, some change from believing "There's nothing I can do about it" to seeing that they have some control over their letter grades. Removing the mystery also removed a barrier between us and our students that we had always felt at report card time. This is a good thing!

Finding 4: Spend Time on What Matters Most

Although it took us time and thought to construct the Learning Maps for each subject area and to refine them over time, we now get to use them over and over again. We find we have stopped fretting so much on a day-to-day basis about assigning letter grades (which we are required to do three or four times per year), and we put more of our energy each and every day into the assessment-*for*-learning practices that make the most difference to learning. (see our e-books on assessment: *Practical Ideas for Assessment for K–3* and *Practical Ideas for Assessment for Grades 4–8*, excerpted from our Voices of Experience series, for grades K–3 and grades 4–8 from Portage & Main Press <www.portageandmainpress.com>.

Finding 5: Show the Link to Learning Standards

Many parents and guardians are more familiar with letter grades that compare students to their classmates rather than letter grades that are based on students' performance in relation to learning standards. Categorizing and recording the three to five Big Ideas (learning standards) as the frame for a Learning Map and concretely showing the link to letter grades is the easiest way we know of to help parents and students come to understand standards-based letter grades.

Finding 6: Talk with Colleagues

For most of our careers, we've arrived at letter grades on our own without talking to anyone. The topic was rarely discussed in school beyond a request that reports were due in the office at a specific time on a specific date. Our experience of talking with colleagues about rethinking how we arrive at letter grades has been the most powerful Pro-D in our careers.

Finding 7: Continue to Change

Something that we keep learning about our profession is that we never get there. Just when we start to think we've arrived, it is time to move forward. Our professional conversations about letter grades are ongoing, and the five-step approach described in this book will continue to change as we work to find more ways to communicate with learners and families effectively. The part that will remain the same for us is that learning needs to be at the core of all that we do.

A Next Step

The next step is completely up to you. We've told you our stories, and now we welcome yours. Feel free to contact us at <www.kathleengregory.com/>.

Appendix 1: Example of Conversion from a Letter Grade to a Percentage

Letter grade and range of percentages*	low range	low range mid-point	middle range	middle range mid-point	high range	high range mid-point
A 86 to 100	86 to 90	88	91 to 95	93	96 to 100	98
B 73 to 85	73 to 76	74.5	77 to 81	79	82 to 85	83.5
C+ 67 to 72	67 to 68	67.5	69 to 70	69.5	71 to 72	71.5
C 60 to 66	60 to 61	60.5	62 to 64	63	65 to 66	65.5
C- 50 to 59	50 to 52	51	53 to 56	54.5	57 to 59	58

*Letter grade and corresponding range of percentages are from BC Ministry of Education.

Appendix 2: Big Ideas for Different Subject Areas

BIG IDEAS

The following Big Ideas are from colleagues teaching in different provinces/states. We've used these examples to show that Big Ideas are often very similar across the country. What differs from place to place are the specific skills/ topics/units that are to be studied.

Mathematics 7

Students

1. know computational skills and concepts **(angles, area, etc.)**
2. use different strategies and approaches to solve tasks
3. see patterns, relationships and relevance
4. communicate/explain and show what they know using materials, math symbols, and terms
5. show a mathematical attitude **(take risks, tolerate ambiguity, persevere, are open-minded)**

Social Studies 6

Students

1. show an understanding of facts, information and vocabulary on topic(s) studied
2. use inquiry/research skills to answer questions and solve problems
3. read and make maps, graphs, and tables
4. make connections between events that happened in the past and their influence on today

Science 8

Students

1. show an understanding of key facts, concepts, and vocabulary on topic(s) studied

2. explain and use the skills of the scientific method

3. describe the impact that science has on the world

Science 2

Students

1. think like a scientist (are curious, observe, ask questions, predict, conduct experiments, record, compare, explain why? how?)

2. describe/explain key information on topic(s) studied

3. show and tell how science is important in the world

French (FSL) 9

Students

1. develop French vocabulary

2. speak in French in everyday conversations in class

3. show an awareness of French culture

Appendix 3: Descriptive Language for Learning Maps

A Performance	B Performance	C Performance
• consistent performance	• Frequent (most-of-the-time) performance	• uneven performance
• completes tasks independently	• may need a bit of prompting to begin a task but can frequently work on his/her own to complete tasks	• demonstrates good grasp in some areas; other areas may need more support
• is intuitive (e.g., when working to solve problems or comprehending text)	• connects to previous learning (e.g., matches prior problems and previous practice)	• needs some type of support, extra time, coaching, re-teaching, or regular prompting to complete tasks
• is willing to try different ways of approaching a problem or of thinking about an issue	• can follow steps	• needs special strategies, for example: a step-by-step map to follow; a template or a guide to fill in; chunked pieces of a task
• perseveres at a task	• can figure out a process or a problem from an example (may need a sample first)	• has a partial grasp of _____
• shows curiosity and can explore further	• is fairly confident	• is beginning to develop skills in some areas
• creates own strategies	• has a good grasp of _____	• provides inconsistent demonstration of understanding
• is willing to go out on a limb	• is developing strength in many areas	• gives some support for ideas/ solutions, and with direction can find more support
• has a strong grasp of _____	• provides accurate explanations (e.g., solutions in math)	
• shows strong skill development in every aspect	• offers relevant support	
• is insightful	• has a strong understanding but may need support in a couple of areas	
• is thoughtful		
• connects to previous learning		
• is confident		
• offers in-depth explanation, shows in-depth comprehension		
• articulates clearly and thoroughly		
• offers relevant and thorough support		
• reasons effectively		

Appendix 4: Parent Brochure on Letter Grades

ARRIVING AT STANDARDS-BASED LETTER GRADES

Understanding and supporting your child's learning and achievement.

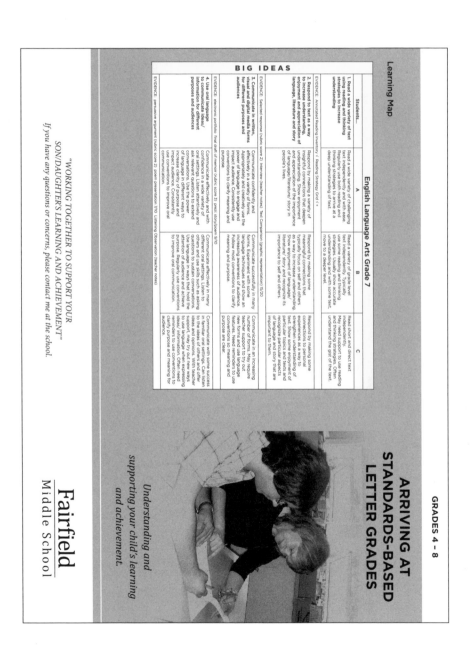

Fairfield
Middle School

"WORKING TOGETHER TO SUPPORT YOUR SON/DAUGHTER'S LEARNING AND ACHIEVEMENT"

If you have any questions or concerns, please contact me at the school.

Learning Map

English Language Arts Grade 7

BIG IDEAS	A	B	C
Students...			
1. Read a wide variety of text using reading and thinking strategies to increase understanding	Read a wide variety of challenging text independently and with ease. Regularly use both reading and thinking strategies to arrive at a deep understanding of text.	Read a variety of grade level text independently. Typically use some reading and thinking strategies to arrive at an understanding and with some text, move to a deeper level.	Read short and direct text independently. May need support to use reading and thinking strategies and understand the gist of the text.
EVIDENCE: Annotated Reading Inventory √ Reading Strategy Grid √ +			
2. Respond to text as a way to increase understanding, enjoyment and appreciation of language, literature and story	Respond by making a variety of insightful connections that deepen understanding. Show enjoyment and appreciation of the importance of language/literature/ story in people's lives.	Respond by making some meaningful connections that typically focus on self and others as a way to increase understanding. Show enjoyment of language/ text. Show some recognition of its importance to self and others.	Respond by making some connections to personal experiences as a way to strengthen understanding. With teacher support to try out particular topics and texts and recognize particular aspects of language and story that are important to them.
EVIDENCE: Selected response (rubric score 2) Interview (teacher notes) Text Comparison (graphic representation) 15/20			
3. Communicate in written, visual and digital media forms for different purposes and audiences	Communicate confidently and effectively in a variety of forms. Appropriately and creatively use the power of language to engage and impact audience. Consistently use conventions to clarify meaning and purpose.	Communicate successfully in many forms. Experiment with some language techniques and show an increasing awareness of audience. Follow most conventions to clarify meaning and purpose.	Communicate in an increasing number of forms. May require new forms and use language features. Need reminders to use conventions so meaning and purpose are clear.
EVIDENCE: electronic portfolio, final draft of memoir (rubric score 3) prezi story/poem 9/10			
4. Use oral language to communicate ideas/ information for different purposes and audiences	Communicate effectively and with confidence in a wide variety of oral settings. Listen attentively and ask relevant question to extend conversations. Use the power of language in different ways to increase clarity of purpose and impact audience. Consistently use conventions to improve oral communication.	Communicate effectively in many different oral settings. Listen to others and use skills such as asking questions to sustain conversations. Use language in ways that hold the attention of audience and achieve purpose. Regularly use conventions to improve oral communication.	Communicate with some success in familiar oral settings. Can listen to the ideas of others and offer ideas and opinions. With teacher support, may try out new ways to use language when expressing ideas/ information. Often need reminders to use conventions to clarify purpose and meaning for audience.
EVIDENCE: persuasive argument (rubric score 2) poem presentation 7/10 Listening Observation (teacher notes)			

What are standards-based letter grades?

Regulations from B.C. Ministry of Education require teachers to write summative reports, including standards-based letter grades.

These letter grades refer to the student's level of performance in relation to learning standards for each subject or course.

How do you arrive at standards-based letter grades?

One approach for arriving at standards-based letter grades is to use a Learning Map which shows

1. the "Big Ideas" (learning standards: what students are expected to learn and be able to do

2. descriptions of learning (at three different levels of quality – A, B, C)

3. specific evidence of learning, which is evaluated by a teacher to determine a letter grade (tests, presentations, projects, teacher observations)

4. highlighted sections of the Learning Map that show how your son/daughter is performing (in relation to grade level expectations for each of the "Big Ideas")

What are some reasons for using a Learning Map?

One reason for using a Learning Map is to show the learning "underneath" the letter grade symbol. When the components of the letter grade are mutually understood by teachers, students and parents, then conversations can become more about the learning and less about numbers, percentages, or grades. Questions such as "What needs to happen to get a better grade?" "She did well on her tests – why did she get a *C*? or "What does it take to get an A in this class?" are all answered by looking at the Learning Map.

The ultimate purpose for using Learning Maps is to show all learners a clear picture of their own strengths, weaknesses, and what they need to do to improve. For many students, a Learning Map removes the mystery of letter grades and students start to see how they can take more responsibility because they see the steps they need to take to improve.

Appendix 5: Conversation Cards

Portage & Main Press, 2014, *Rethinking Letter Grades*, BLM, ISBN: 978-1-55379-537-7

CONVERSATION CARDS
(one person at a time)

_____

1. pick a conversation card
2. read it aloud
3. say your thoughts (e.g. agree, disagree, make connections, give personal experiences)
4. invite comments or questions from others in your group (or not)
5. next person repeats steps

What's an "A"?

In BC it's 86 – 100 %

In Ontario it's 80 – 100 %

In Maine it's 90 – 100 %

So, What is an "A" ?

80? Or 86? Or 90%? ....of WHAT?

"...much of what is done in the name of assessment may be effective for grade books – but for learning, it does nothing."

Black and Wiliam

Computerized grading programs and electronic gradebooks yield neither greater objectivity nor enhanced fairness.

At best, they offer a tool for manipulating data...they do not lessen the challenge involved in assigning grades that accurately and fairly reflect students' achievement and level of performance.

Tom Guskey. *How's My Kid Doing?*
p. 108

To what extent do you believe that the letter grades you currently assign are an accurate representation of your students' learning in relation to required learning standards?

The traditional method of scoring classroom assessments using points or percentages usurps the evaluation process...People rarely question whether percentage scores truly represent student learning. They simply assume the scores are an accurate reflection of students' understanding and/or performance.

Teacher judgment is replaced by 'the power of the points'

Robert Marzano. *Transforming Classroom Grading* p. 80

To what extent do you believe students and parents should know how you arrive at letter grades?

No assessment or evaluation technique is capable of offering absolute truth.

...test scores, teacher observations, teacher or self-ratings – even simple checklists – are, at best, approximations of reality and must be interpreted cautiously and within the context of the teacher's experiences and knowledge about the individual students and the learning situation.

Sharon Jeroski. *Enhancing and Evaluating Oral Communication in the Secondary Grades* p. 3

Portage & Main Press, 2014, *Rethinking Letter Grades*, BLM, ISBN: 978-1-55379-537-7

Tell of a time when numbers underestimated or overestimated the learning of one of your students.

Criterion-referenced standards (for grading) involve the use of clearly stated descriptions of performance that differentiate various levels of quality.

...This means that teachers must identify what they want their students to learn, what evidence they will use to verify that learning, and what criteria will be used to judge that evidence.

Tom Guskey. *How's My Kid Doing?* p. 28

If a student comes to you and asks "how do I move from a B to an A?", how have you responded? How would you like to respond?

Virtually all of the criticisms (on grading) focus on one or more of three problem areas:

Teachers consider many factors other than academic achievement when they assign grades

Teachers weight assessments differently

Teachers misinterpret single scores on classroom assessments by mixing different types of knowledge and skills into single scores.

Robert Marzano. *Transforming Classroom Grading* p. 80

Appendix 6: Article. "Arriving at Letter Grades: Get Closer to the Learning"

"I've collected lots of information on students, but I don't know how to put it all together into a letter grade. I've got test scores, project marks, percentages, rubric scales 1-2-3, checks and pluses and minuses, self and peer assessment, checklists, comments, my observations, homework scores, portfolios, journals … and more!! I know we are supposed to be giving letter grades that are criterion-referenced, but I am not exactly sure what that means either. How can I take all of this information and come up with a single letter grade?"

Many of our conversations for the last decade have included questions about reporting, such as: What gets added in? Does effort count? What do you do when students don't hand work in on time? What does an *A* mean anyway?

Step one:

Look at your provincial curriculum requirements, which are often called learning standards or outcomes (what students are expected to learn and be able to do) and determine the three to five big, overriding ideas that you are required to teach in your subject area.

For example:

Math – Gr. 7
Students will …

- know computational skills/concepts (angles, area, etc.)

- use different strategies and approaches to solve tasks (how students approach mathematical tasks, e.g., do they do so independently, what varied strategies do they use, do they reflect to tell when they are on or off track, do they seek support if they need it, do they use manipulatives as a strategy, etc.)

- see patterns, relationship, and relevance (students see and use patterns, interpret them, describe and explain)

- communicate/explain and show what they know using materials, math symbols and terms (can explain how they arrived at answers; show, represent, and use terms correctly; use symbols correctly)
- show a mathematical attitude (take risks, tolerate ambiguity, persevere with short-term tasks as well as open-ended complex tasks; are self-motivated to figure out an answer.)

Step two:

Record these Big Ideas on the left-hand side of the paper. Then, write three levels of descriptions for each Big Idea. Words that describe frequency (*consistently, usually, occasionally*) and level of support (*independently, with some support, with regular or one-on-one support*) can often show distinctions between levels. These descriptions of performance will show a range of performance from satisfactory (*C*) to excellent (*A*) performance.

Step three:

For each Big Idea, decide what assessment information you will be collecting as evidence for the learning. This information may be from observing students, from students' work products, and from conversations with students. Record the specific type of evidence you will be using on the Learning Map.

Step four:

Look at your assessment information (evidence) for each students' performance to get an overall picture. Then *match*, rather than add up, the assessment information with the description that is the closest "fit" for each Big Idea. Circle or highlight one of these descriptions for each Big Idea.

Step five:

From the patterns/trends that are shown on the Learning Map, determine which grade to assign. Some patterns are very clear and indicate an obvious letter grade. Other performances are "all over the map." In this case, teachers use their own professional judgment to determine, in relation to the outcomes, the letter grade that reflects the most consistent pattern of student achievement.

QUESTION AND RESPONSES

Q: We have to give percentages. How can that work with this process?

R: One way teachers deal with percentages is to arrive at a letter grade *first* and then decide on the percentage. For example, look at the range of the percent for an *A* letter grade (86%–100%) and decide on a low (86%–89%), a mid (90%–95%) or high (96%–100%) percentage range.

Again, teachers use the assessment information and their professional judgment to decide if the student's performance is in the high, middle, or low portion of the range.

> Rarely do people question whether percentage scores truly represent students learning. They simply assume the scores are an accurate reflection of students' understanding and performance. Teacher do not determine whether the difference between the percentage scores of 70 to 75 represents the same difference in achievement indicated by the difference between 90 and 95. To coin a phrase, teacher judgment is replaced by the 'power of the points' (Marzano 2000, 86).

Q: Isn't this approach very subjective?

R: All assessment and evaluation is subjective to some degree. To help us be as accurate as possible, we find that it is important to include observation, student products, and conversations as evidence of learning in relation to standards (outcomes). When we look at these multiple measures of students' performance, these three perspectives help us find an "approximation of reality." Whether we like it or not, assessment and evaluation is still "a complex process of human judgment" (Sutton 1997, 10).

> "No assessment or evaluation technique is capable of offering absolute truth. Standardized test scores, teacher observations, teacher or self ratings – even simple checklists – are, at best, approximations of reality and must be interpreted cautiously and within the context of teacher's experience and knowledge about the individual student and the learning situation" (Jeroski 1989, 33).

Q. My biggest question is: how can I justify my letter grades to parents?

What we have found is that most parents want to know the grade, and also, what needs to be improved (What does he/she need to work on at home?) The description of the letter grades links the letter grades to the learning, and parents can see exactly what their son/daughter needs to do to obtain a higher grade. We also find that when our students have been involved in the assessment process by talking with their parents about their learning and showing evidence of their learning and progress during a conference, we rarely are asked to justify letter grades to these parents.

Q: Our electronic grade-book program requires a percentage and then we fit numbers into each of the bins and weight each assignment. What can we do?

We recognize how seductive technology can be to both educators and parents; it gives off the aura of accurate, clean, complete, and unquestionable information on achievement. It can also hide the complexity of assessment and learning, which is often messy, non-linear, and ambiguous. We find that as we move towards using standards-based letter grades, we have a great deal of evidence that does not "fit" into a numerical form, and we no longer feel comfortable inputting numbers, weighting them, and accepting the resulting grade (computed electronically) as an accurate reporting of students' performance. We want to have a valid picture of student achievement – one that recognizes all aspects of student performance. We adapt the technology so it is useful for us and supports us in tracking the evidence we collect.

> Above all, we have to recognize that teachers' professional judgments will always be an essential part of the grading process. Teachers at all levels must make carefully reasoned decisions about the purpose of the grade, the components that will be included in determining the grade, how those components will be combined and summarized and what format will be used in reporting those summaries. ... In the end, teachers must still decide what grade offers the most accurate and fairest description of each student's achievement and level of performance over a particular period. (Guskey 2002, 111).

> Computerized grading programs and electronic gradebooks yield neither greater objectivity nor enhanced fairness. At best, they offer a tool for manipulating data... they do not lessen the challenge involved in assigning grades that accurately and fairly reflect students' achievement and level of performance. (Guskey 2002, 107)

References

Guskey, Thomas. *How's My Kid Doing?* San Francisco: Jossey-Bass, 2002.

Jeroski, Sharon. *Enhancing and Evaluating Oral Communication in the Secondary Grades.* Victoria: B.C. Ministry of Education, 1989.

Marzano, Robert. *Transforming Classroom Grading.* Alexandria, VA: ASCD, 2000.

Sutton, Ruth. *The Learning School.* Salford, England: RS Publications, 1997.